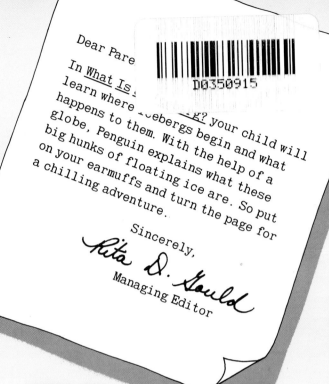

Dear Pare...

In What Is ... ...g? your child will
learn where ...cebergs begin and what
happens to them. With the help of a
globe, Penguin explains what these
big hunks of floating ice are. So put
on your earmuffs and turn the page for
a chilling adventure.

Sincerely,

Rita D. Gould

Managing Editor

FAMILY FUN

- Make your own icebergs. Fill a glass
  with water to about 1 inch from the
  rim. Place an ice cube in the water.
  Help your child note how only a small
  part of the ice cube is above the water.
  Most of the ice cube stays underwater—
  just like an iceberg. Or freeze water in
  several different-shaped containers.
  Place the frozen shapes in a large bowl
  of water. Have your child count the
  "icebergs."

READ MORE ABOUT IT

- *Why Does It Float?*
- *Why Is It Cold?*

This book is a presentation of Weekly Reader
Books. Weekly Reader Books offers book
clubs for children from preschool through high
school. For further information write to:
WEEKLY READER BOOKS, 4343 Equity Drive,
Columbus, Ohio 43228

This edition is published by arrangement
with Checkerboard Press.

Weekly Reader is a federally registered trademark
of Field Publications.

WEEKLY READER BOOKS presents

What Is an Iceberg?

A **Just Ask**™ Book

Hi, my name is
Christopher!

by Chris Arvetis
and Carole Palmer

illustrated by
Susan Swan

FIELD PUBLICATIONS
MIDDLETOWN, CT.

Let's ask the penguins
who live here.
They can show you where
an iceberg comes from.
Then you'll know
what it is.

Can you tell Christopher about an iceberg?

Sure, we'll use our globe.
I have marked the North Pole
with an X.
At the opposite end is the
South Pole.
It is very cold at the North
and South Poles.
The snow piles up on the land.
It gets thicker and thicker.

Even in summer it stays cold.
It does not get warm enough
for the snow to melt.

Over the years, the thick
snow turns into ice.

This large chunk of ice and
snow is called a glacier.

Let's say it together—
GLA-CIER.

As the glacier gets bigger and bigger, it moves forward. The weight of all the ice and snow causes it to move. The top layers move over the heavier bottom layers.

The glacier moves very slowly—
too slowly for you to see.
As it moves, the heavy ice
digs up rocks and boulders.
The glacier pushes anything
in its way.

The glacier moves over
the land to the ocean.
There, large pieces of the
glacier are pushed out
into the water.
When these pieces break off,
they become icebergs.
Look at that big one!

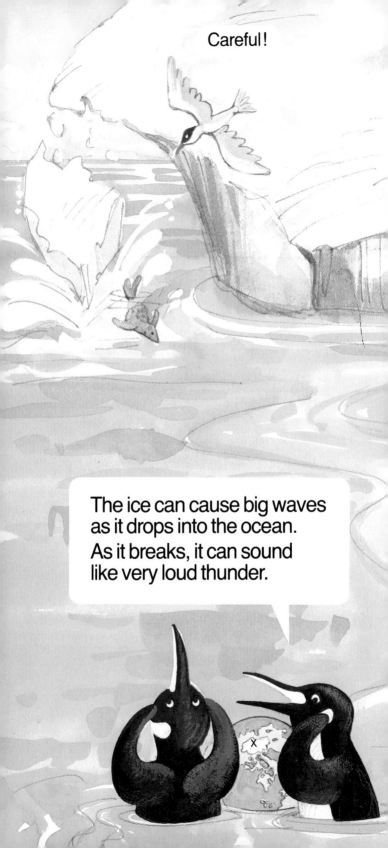

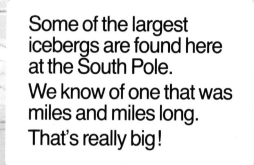

Some of the largest icebergs are found here at the South Pole.

We know of one that was miles and miles long.

That's really big!

The icebergs float far out into the oceans.
They float to places that are warmer.
Then the icebergs break up into smaller pieces.

The further the iceberg pieces float, the warmer the weather gets.
The warm weather causes the small chunks to melt.

Now let's look closely
at an iceberg.

The part we see floating
above the water is the
smallest part.

The biggest part is under
the water.

People have said that
icebergs look like
mountains, towers,
or castles.

Icebergs are very
beautiful sights.

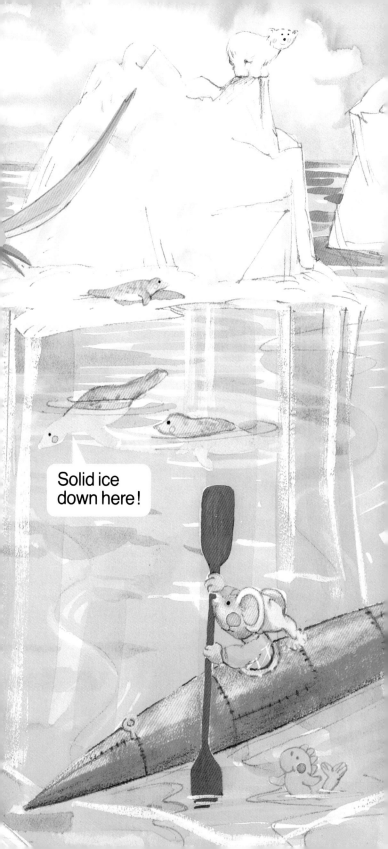

Icebergs can also
be very dangerous.
Ships that sail the ocean
must watch for icebergs.
A ship might easily sink
if it hits an iceberg.

Special people on big ships look for icebergs.
They let other ships know where the icebergs are.

And now you know.
Icebergs are large chunks of ice
that have broken off from glaciers.
The icebergs make interesting and
beautiful shapes in the ocean.
But they can be dangerous, too.